LONDON MIDLAND STEAM in action

LONDON MIDLAND STEAM IN ACTION

W. A. Blake

D. BRADFORD BARTON LIMITED

Frontispiece: Compound 4-4-0 No. 40932 appears to be working much harder than the 'Jubilee', No. 45615 *Malay States* that she is piloting on this St. Pancras—Bradford express passing Bedford in April 1952. These were the two classes, above all others, best remembered for fast passenger work on the former Midland lines.   [P. J. Lynch]

© *copyright D. Bradford Barton Ltd 1974*

printed in Great Britain by Chapel River Press (IPC Printers), Andover, Hants
for the publishers

D. BRADFORD BARTON LTD · Trethellan House · Truro · Cornwall · England

introduction

The L.M.S., serving the Midlands, the industrial north-west and Scotland, as well as providing the principal link with Ireland, was the richest and most powerful of the pre-Nationalisation companies. At Nationalisation, its dominance became apparent and for something like a decade the L.M.S. look changed surprisingly little on what had become the London Midland Region of British Railways. On other Regions, the effect was more marked, not least by the introduction of B.R. Standard classes of locomotives which were, in effect, up-dated designs of obvious L.M.S. parentage. That the honour of being the last stronghold of steam on Britain's main lines fell to the L.M. Region was not surprising—a reflection of its dominance and its well-ordered range of relatively up-to-date motive power that had been inherited from the L.M.S.R. in 1948, twenty years before. Thus the illustrations in this volume, although all taken in post-Nationalisation years, could well be of the old L.M.S.R., except in a few details. Not surprisingly, steam on these former lines has a following among enthusiasts that is only exceeded by that of the former Great Western, where fierce loyalties are proverbial. It is hoped that these pages portray something of the character of the L.M.S.; we all have our favourite memories, all of which are, alas, now fading with the passage of time—perhaps a 'Jubilee', behind time and being worked to the limit, on the climb to Ais Gill; an ageing Class 2P 4-4-0 working out her time on three-coach locals out of Bedford; a 'Duchess'—finest of them all—sweeping down Madeley bank with 'The Royal Scot'; or the sight and sound of an 8F 2-8-0 slogging up to Standedge tunnel with a heavy load of Yorkshire coal. Even the Class Fives, ten years ago so commonplace they were barely given a second glance, would now be a noble sight heading a rake of well-worn stock on one of the once innumerable summer excursions to Blackpool or Llandudno. Memories remain, too, of the sounds as well as the sights, ranging from the quick three-cylinder exhaust beat of a rebuilt 'Royal Scot' at speed, the wheezy 1 2 3 4 rhythm of a G2 0-8-0 goods from L.N.W.R. days, or the clank of rods on an elderly 'Patriot'. Alas, except at a few places such as Dinting, Carnforth and Tyseley, L.M. steam is now gone, replaced on the West Coast main line by faceless electrics and elsewhere by anonymous diesels.

One of Sir William Stanier's early batch of Pacifics, No. 46203 *Princess Margaret Rose,*
north of Kensal Green in June 1954 with the down 'Mid-day Scot'. This express, in-
augurated in 1927, was a regular 'Princess' turn in post-war years.   [S. Creer]

Scenes at South Kenton, August 1950: Rebuilt 'Patriot' Class No. 45522 *Prestatyn* with
down engineers' special, and *below* No. 46158 *The Loyal Regiment* heading towards Eusto
with an express from Carlisle.   [Derek Cros

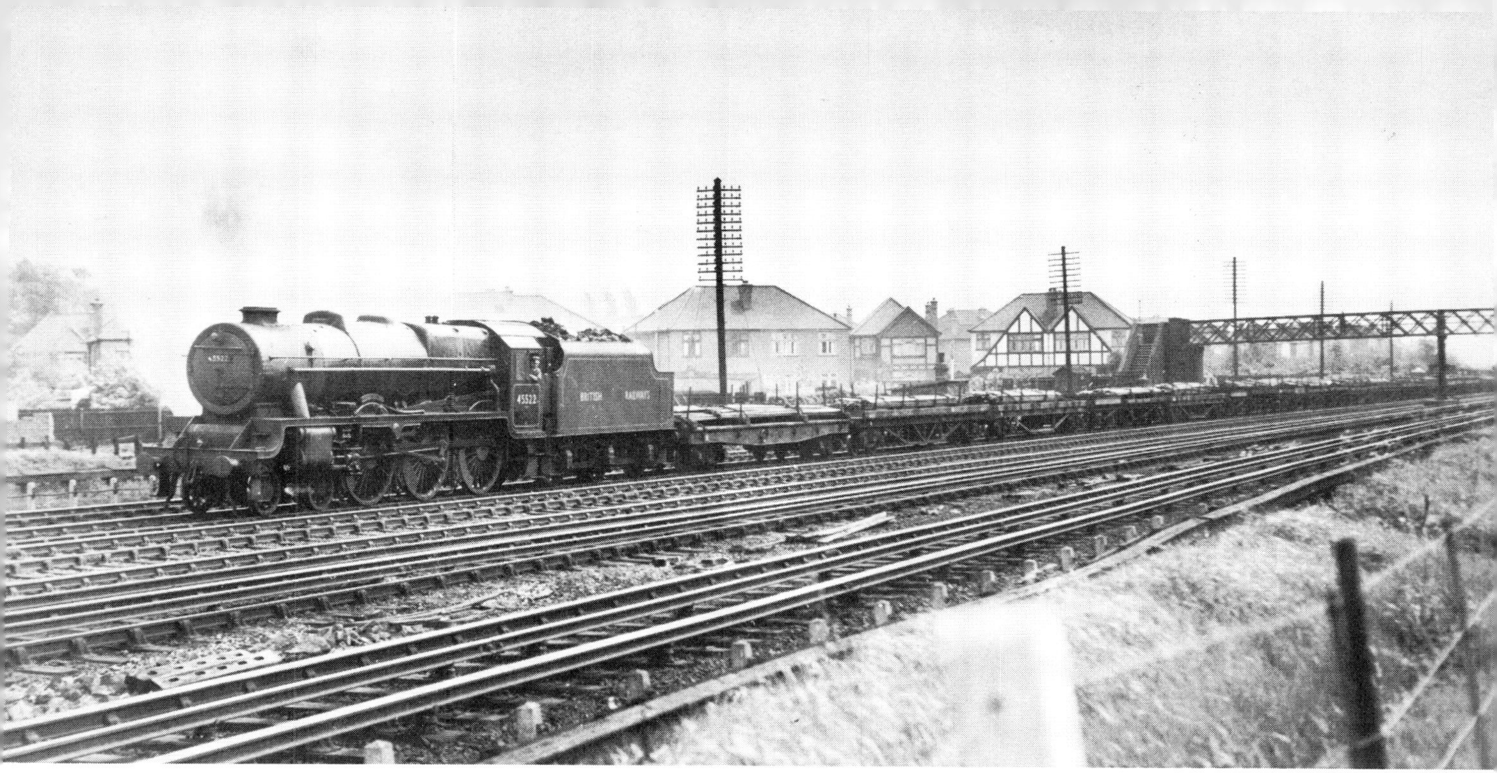
45522
BRITISH RAILWAYS

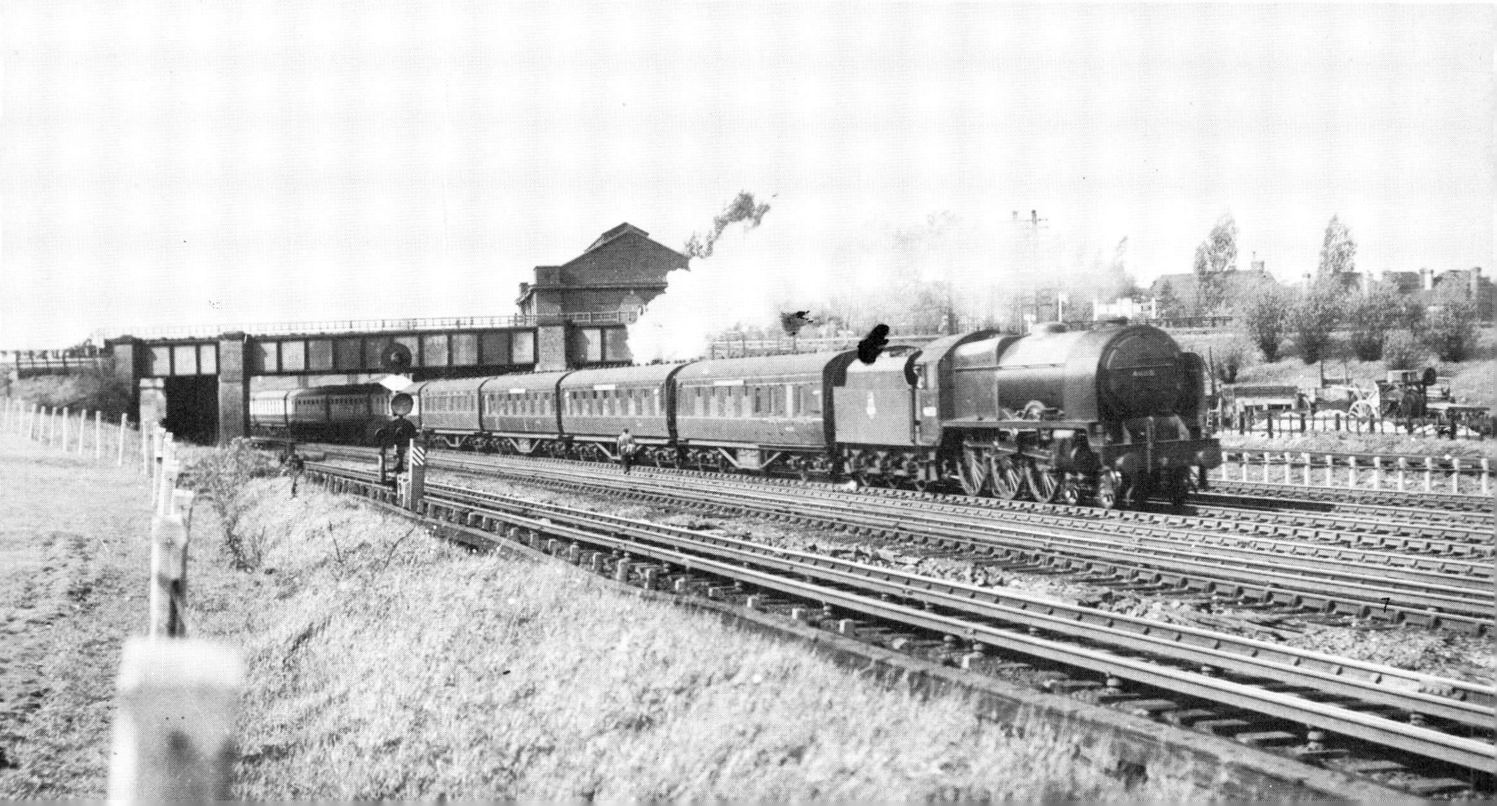

'Jubilee' Class No. 45733 *Novelty* makes light work of an eight coach Euston–Northampton train through Kenton, August 1964. She was one of the 64 in the class withdrawn that year.

[P. J. Lynch]

Headstone Lane on a sunny June day in 1959: No. 46203 *Princess Margaret Rose* again overtaking one of the Watford electrics, at the head of the up 'Merseyside Express'. Withdrawn from service in 1962, this fine locomotive was saved from the scrapyard and bought by Messrs. Butlin for display at their Pwllheli holiday camp. *Below*; Ex-L.N.W.R. 'G2' 0-8-0 No. 49441 drifts south down the 1 in 339 with a long freight on the slow line for Camden.

[Derek Cross]

Another 'G2A', No. 49049, approaching Watford with a freight from Bletchley in September 1954. These sturdy 0-8-0's—turned out literally by the thousand at Crewe—are remembered with great affection, not least for their distinctive exhaust beat. Despite their age, they lasted in some numbers until 1960 or so, the last disappearing in 1964.

[S. Creer]

The 1950's saw rather a spate of express naming on the part of British Railways in an endeavour to recaptu[re] something of their former popular appeal with the travelling public. 'The Shamrock' was one of thes[e] christened in 1954 as one of the principal expresses to Liverpool (Lime Street), along with the long esta[b]lished 'Merseyside Express', and 'The Red Rose' which dated from 1951. It is seen here leaving Watfor[d] tunnel in September 1954 hauled by No. 46110 *Grenadier Guardsman*.

[S. Cree[r]]

THE
SHAMROCK
46110

THE
MANCUNIAN
45506

Ex-L.N.W.R. Class 2F 0-6-2T 'Coal Tank' No. 58887 on a Dunstable branch train at Leighton Buzzard, July 1951. On the left is 'G2' 0-8-0 No. 49287, both locomotives being from Bletchley shed. [P. J. Lynch]

ll in her original parallel-boiler condition, Royal Scot No. 46156 *The South Wales rderer* eases the 2.30 p.m. Euston to Liverpool express from the main to the slow down e at Watford South, due to engineers' possession of the main line tunnels, 22 September 52. [P. J. Lynch]

e of the named 'Patriots', No. 45506 *The Royal Pioneer Corps* slams through Leighton zzard with the up 'Mancunian' in May 1952. Though not the equal of the bigger class, se 'Baby Scots' could give a good account of themselves and on occasion were led on for some heavy express and excursion turns. [P. J. Lynch]

Rebuilt 'Patriot' No 45521 *Rhyl* leaves a haze of exhaust over Stafford as she starts away past the locomotive shed with a down express on 24 May 1958.

[P. J. Shoesmith]

he magnificent 'Duchess' Class were the prima donnas on the Anglo-Scottish services ut of Euston and the finest express locomotives ever to see service in Britain—free eaming, fast running, trouble-free and capable of taking Shap in their stride. Here o. 46251 *City of Nottingham* heads through Bletchley with the up 'Royal Scot' in April 60; and (*below*) is No. 46243 *City of Lancaster* beneath the new flyover at Bletchley with a arcels train bound for Carlisle.

[S. Creer]

In terms of looks, it was the 'Duchesses' for power and the 'Princesses' for grace—and many consider the latter had the finest lines of any British express locomotive design. No. 46208 *Princess Helena Victoria* is seen at speed near Welton with a sixteen-coach Euston–Liverpool express. In June 1960, the motorway alongside is curiously bare of traffic by the standards of the 70's.

[Derek Cross]

Another heavy parcels train for a Stanier 2-6-0—one that would daunt many a lesser breed of British mogul—on Madeley Bank, south of Crewe. Classed 5F by the L.M.S., they were in fact used for any and every kind of duty. On North Wales excursion trains in particular they put in some very fast working and despite smaller (5ft 6in) coupled wheels, they had a turn of speed rivalling the Class 5s.   [Derek Cross]

he Stanier 2-6-0s, introduced from 1933 onwards, were successful engines and performed a wide range of uties but were overshadowed by the Class 5 4-6-0s which followed them in 1934. Only forty were built, ompared to the 800 or so Class 5s, making these moguls comparative rarities—especially so as they were idely scattered on the L.M.S. and the L.M. Region. Here, No. 42953 works a parcels past Welton towards rewe in June 1960.   [Derek Cross]

Displaced by diesels on the West Coast main line, the 'Duchesses' spent their last couple of years on services that would formerly have been beneath their dignity. No. 46233 *Duchess of Sutherland* at Birmingham (New Street) with an express for Euston, 1963.
[S. Creer]

deley Bank, south of Crewe, is nine miles varying from 1 in 348 to 1 in 177, which today's electrics barely tice but which in steam days was a well known stretch for losing or making up time. In July 1949 'Patriot' ss No. 45517 *above* heads south with a fitted freight, and is about to pass a Rebuilt 'Royal Scot'—still hout smoke deflectors—on 'The Lakes Express'. *Below:* No. 46233 *Duchess of Sutherland* on 'The Royal ot' in September 1960, at a time when this was run with a limited load of eight coaches to minimise the ays incurred by electrification work south of Crewe.
[Derek Cross]

Ex-M.R. Class 3F 0-6-0 No. 43521 shunting at Stratford-on-Avon in October 1951. Three of this long-lived class, originally dating from 1885, survived to 1964, No. 43521 herself lasting to 1963. [B. A. Butt]

Class 4F 0-6-0 No. 44587, paired with a high-sided tender, on a freight near Stratford-on-Avon. [B. A. B

Smoke and sunlight at the western end of the Midland section of Birmingham (New Street) in May 1957. Class 2P 4-4-0 No. 40332 is about to depart with a train to Gloucester. [P. J. Lynch]

e evening rush-hour
the Midland side of
mingham (New
eet) on 4 April 1963.
. 42421 starts the
0 p.m. to Redditch
a Class 5 waits with
Gloucester train.

[P. J. Shoesmith]

ass 4F No. 44184,
th express head-
mps up, substitutes
the usual 'Jubilee'
an express to the
uth-west, at King's
orton on 28 July 1959,
e peak Saturday for
dlands holiday
ffic.

[P. J. Shoesmith]

A young 'train-spotter' watches Class 5 No. 44757 heading an express through King's Norton in May 1958. This was one of three of the class with the combination of Caprotti valve gear, a lowered running plate and double chimney. [P. J. Shoesmith]

Ivatt-designed Class 2 mogul No. 46443 arrives at Redditch with an evening local train from Birmingham, June 1963. She is now preserved on the Severn Valley Railway. [P. J. Shoesmith]

The northbound 'Pines Express', from Bournemouth, struggles up the unremitting 1 in 37 of Lickey on a damp August day in 1960. With eleven bogies behind her tender, 'Patriot' No. 45504 *Royal Signals* needs all the help she can from the banker in the rear.   [Derek Cross]

The combined efforts of a Compound 4-4-0, a 'Jubilee' 4-6-0 plus a Class 5 in the rea[r] lift a long Cardiff–Newcastle train up Lickey, the sound being audible miles away acros[s] the fields.   [S. Cree[r]

One of the 'Jubilee' class draws away from Gloucester past Tramway Junction with a nort[h]bound train, passing a W.R. 0-4-2T on the Chalford auto-train.   [P. J. Lynch]

A southbound parcels hurries through Lansdown Junction, Cheltenham, behind No. 45561 *Saskatchewan* in June 1964. The grimy state of this 'Jubilee'—in contrast to the new coach coupled next to the tender—is evidence of the shortage of shed-cleaners and maintenance staff that marked the last few years of steam operation, particularly in the Midlands area.

[Derek Cross]

Class 2P 0-4-4T No. 41900 enters the 'cottage orne'-style station at Ripple on the As church–Malvern branch, by this time cut back to Upton-on-Severn, on 4 July 1959, with train from Upton-on-Severn to Ashchurch. This branch has long since closed, but that time Ripple enjoyed a service of two trains a day in each direction, with a third one Saturdays.

[P. J. Shoesmit

41900
RIPPLE

The Somerset & Dorset was
an outpost of the Midland
typified by this double-
heading of a Class 2P 4-4-0
and Class 4F 0-6-0 of Derby
origin. The setting is the
Midford valley, with a train
from Bath to Templecombe.
[Derek Cross]

Two generations of freight
engines on the S. & D. at
Midford; No. 53808, of the
well-loved S. & D. J. 2-8-0
Class 7F, and Stanier Class
8F No. 48737. The latter was
one of the war–time batch
built by the L.N.E.R.
[Derek Cross]

2-8-0 No. 53806 crossing
Midford viaduct with a goods
from Evercreech to Bath.
She was one of the five in
this class built in 1925, and
was withdrawn in 1964.
[Derek Cross]

'Jubilee' No. 45577 *Bengal* on a three-coach Shrewsbury–Swansea stopping train amid rural scenery near Knighton on the Central Wales line. This route, through Llandrindod Wells, traverses a beautiful but little known part of the Principality.   [Derek Cross]

Another stopper on the Central Wales line, on the curve by Knucklas Viaduct in 1964. This ornate 13-arch structure crossed the river Teme, and was one of the most photogenic features of this line, which leaves the main Hereford–Shrewsbury north-to-west route at Craven Arms. Deserted Knucklas Halt in the foreground tells its own story of the lack of passenger traffic by this date.   [Derek Cross]

Stanier Class 8F No. 48761 comes slowly round the curve from the Central Wales line and joins the main line from Hereford. The train is a freight from Swansea destined for Coleham yard at Shrewsbury.

[Derek Cross]

Craven Arms, and a classic study in late evening sunlight of an 8F, No. 48409, drifting south with coal empties. Note the lower quadrant signals on this joint G.W./L.M.S. route along the borders of Wales.
[Derek Cross]

No. 46202 'Turbomotive' was withdrawn in 1951 and re-appeared next year rebuilt as a conventional locomotive named *Princess Anne*. Crewe to Shrewsbury turns were used by Crewe works for running in, and she is seen here about to leave Shrewsbury on 23 August 1952. About six weeks later, No. 46202 was destroyed in the tragic disaster at Harrow.

[P. J. Shoesmith]

2-8-0 No. 48418 clumps through Shrewsbury with a train of petroleum tank wagons from Ellesmere Port. She was one of the class built at Swindon during the war years.

[Derek Cross]

The workhorse of the L.M.S.R. was of course the Class 5 4-6-0, introduced in 1934, and built in vast numbers for mixed traffic duties from then on. They are probably the best memorial to Sir William Stanier's outstanding abilities as a locomotive designer. Several variants were built, with Caprotti or Stephenson valve gear instead of the usual Walschaerts, and some with roller bearings and double chimneys. No. 44766, seen here leaving Chester with an excursion to Llandudno, was one of those with the last named two features allied to normal Walschaerts gear.   [J. R. Carter]

'Jubilee' No. 45671 *Prince Rupert* at the head of a partly fitted freight negotiating the series of cuttings, short tunnels and over–bridges after leaving Chester station on the North Wales line. This section has quadruple track as far as Saltney Junction where the W.R. lines to Shrewsbury—seen above on the right—leave those of the L.M. Region to Holyhead. Note the banner 'repeater' signal beside the down W.R. line, necessary on account of the bad visibility due to the smoke and gloom along this section.　　　　[J. R. Carter]

Ex-L.&Y. 0-6-0 No. 52358—still with L.M.S. lettering on her tender—passing over Flint
water-troughs on the North Wales coast line in September 1950.   [Derek Cross]

The Class Fives were widely used on passenger work in North Wales and when the excursion traffic was at its height each summer they congregated at Llandudno Junction by the dozen, from sheds everywhere in the Midlands, the Potteries, and the industrial north-west. Here, one of the class leans to the curve off the Britannia tubular bridge spanning Menai Straits, Manchester-bound with a train from Holyhead.

[S. Creer]

At Llandudno Junction, the lines to Llandudno curve sharply north alongside the Conway estuary away from those continuing to Holyhead. On this curve, a DMU on the coastal shuttle service from Rhyl passes an Ivatt Class 2 2-6-0 bound for the Junction sidings with a short pick-up goods.

[Derek Cross]

Bangor in July 1965, and a Fairburn 2-6-4T heads out with a stopping train for Llandudno Junction.
[Malcolm Dunnett]

The ubiquitous Class 5;
beneath the walls of Conway
Castle where a brave attempt
was made to blend the
architecture of a nineteenth
century railway with that of a
castle dating from Edward I.
[Malcolm Dunnett]

At one time weight restrictions barred the heavier Pacifics from North Wales but they were later permitted to work through to Holyhead, replacing the 'Royal Scots' on duties such as 'The Irish Mail'. Here No. 46222 *Queen Mary* draws away from Llandudno Junction in July 1963 with an extra, returning to the Midlands. She was the third locomotive in the class, and built originally with streamlined casing.   [J. R. Carter]

2-6-4T on the Bangor–Llandudno Junction service draws away from Conway station on the sharp ¿rve under part of the outer ramparts of the castle. Note the unusual signal post carrying arms for the ¿wn home and up starter.   [Derek Cross]

Stanier 2-6-2T No. 40077 on station pilot duties at Llandudno Junction in 1960, marshalling stock for a Manchester train. The main batch of these smart little machines was withdrawn from L.M.Region stock in 1961, ousted by soul-less DMUs.

[P. J. Lynch]

40034

In stark contrast to the lonely Welsh countryside opposite, a scene at Crewe beneath a complex of overhead electrification wires and supports. 'Jubilee' No. 45671 *Prince Rupert,* featured already in these pages, draws away, resplendent in maroon livery and in a condition that does credit to the cleaners on her home shed.

[J. R. Carter]

Another of the handsome little taper-boiler 2-6-2Ts produced at Crewe, No. 40085, at Penrhyndeudraeth near Portmadoc in June 1960. She is on a Western Region working from Aberystwyth tp Pwllheli, although based on Llandudno Junction shed. These Class 3P tanks were used on various of the North Wales branches, notably the one to Blaenau Ffestiniog and from Caernarvon to Afonwen.

[Derek Cross]

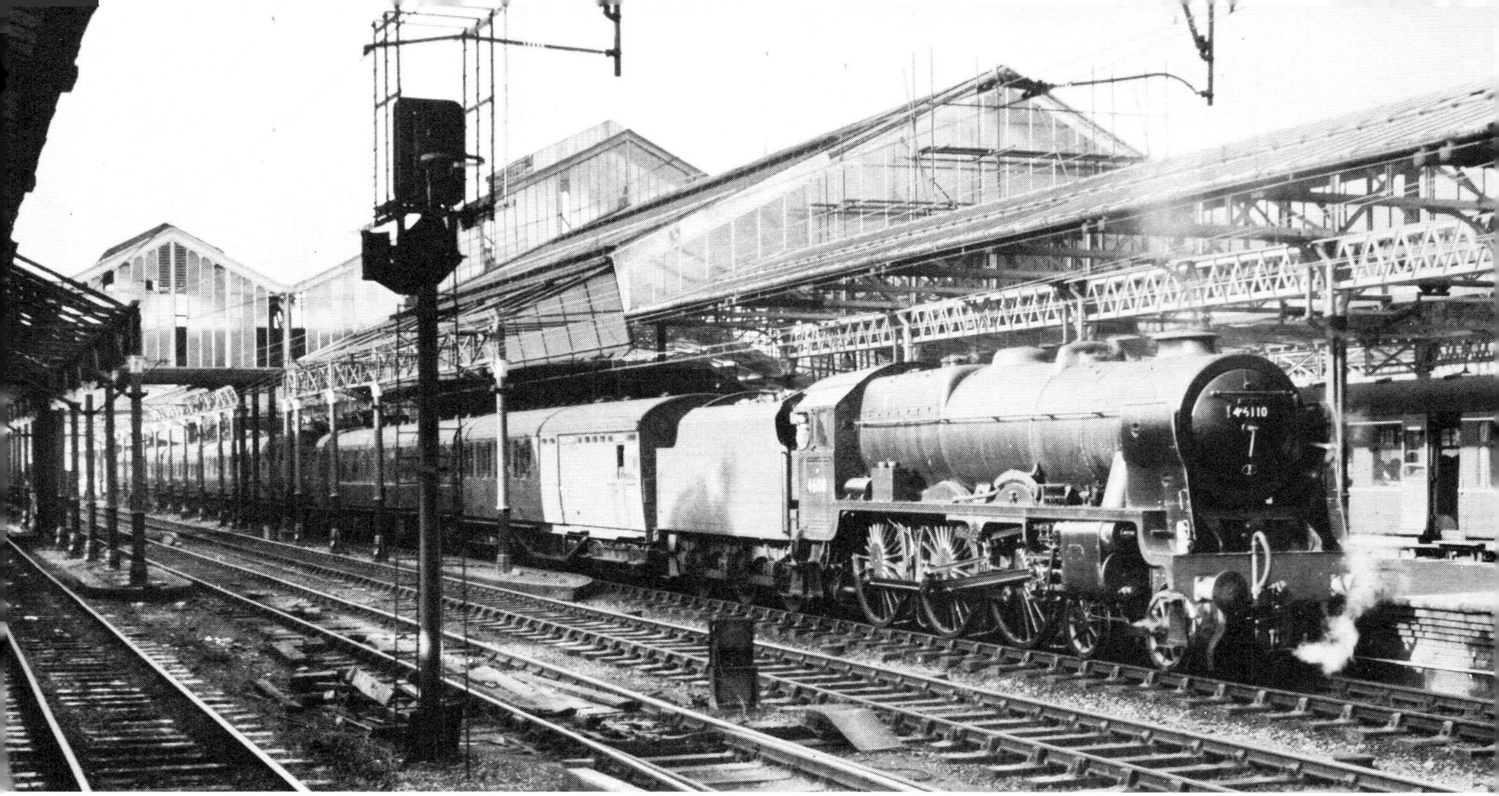

Class 5s on freight duties pass on the main line south of Warrington, close by the bridge (*left*) over the Manchester Ship Canal. [J. R. Carter]

ebuilt 'Royal Scot' No. 46110 *Grenadier Guardsman* at Crewe in eptember 1960 with a Manchester–Birmingham express. [Derek Cross]

ne south end of Warrington (Bank Quay) in June 1955, long before e coming of any efficient but uninteresting electrics; an ex-L.N.W.R. 8-0 plods towards Wigan with a freight from Crewe. [P. J. Lynch]

Class 5 No. 45311 makes a rousing start from Manchester (Exchange) with a train for Barrow in 1962.

[J. R. Carter]

A Liverpool–Glasgow
express, headed by
Rebuilt 'Patriot' No.
45512 *Bunsen,* held at
the signals south of
Carnforth, August 1964.
[Derek Cross]

48476
78

A magnificent 15-arm signal gantry at the north end of Preston makes a frame for Class 8F No. 48476 at the head of a freight from Ribble Sidings to Heysham. The date is June 1968 and steam on the London Midland is near an end.					[Derek Cross]

Snowplough-fitted Class 5 No. 45126 picks up water on Dillicar troughs south of Tebay whilst working the morning Crewe–Carlisle parcels. Normally one of the Crewe (North) allocation of 'Duchesses' was rostered to this train, which was beyond the abilities of even the best Class 5.

[J. R. Carter]

On the severe five mile climb to Shap summit from Tebay, the great majority of north-bound trains received banking assistance. In post-war years 2-6-4 tanks, of the parallel-boiler Fowler design or the later ones by Stanier or Fairburn, were principally made use of for this duty. No. 42665, of the Stanier two-cylinder variety, helps a freight up the 1 in 75 near Scout Green towards the summit.   [P. H. Wells]

On a cold day in November 1965, a Class 5 and one of Tebay's 2-6-4T bankers lay trails of smoke and steam across the fells as they tackle Shap, with a northbound mixed goods. [P. H. Wells]

A train of bogie wagons carrying concrete sleeper track on Shap, with two Class 8Fs at the head and 2-6-4T—apparently working hardest—behind. [P. H. Wel

Down the 1 in 75 past the tiny Scout Green signalbox, No. 46105 *Cameron Highlander* at speed with a Glasgo –Euston express in 1950. The extremely tall ex-L.N.W.R. signal was needed here for sighting purposes increase the braking distance available for southbound expresses running fast downhill. [B. A. Bu

One of the 'Duchess' Class going well at the approach to Tebay loop crossing the river Lune, in 1951. The M6 motorway has opened up the scenic Lune gorge from this point down towards Low Gill and has largely spoiled its former character. Electrification of this line has further destroyed its image. [B. A. Butt]

South of Low Gill, Class 4F 0-6-0 No. 44469 hammers north with a freight in October 1956. This was princip loaded with coke, being worked from the Barrow-in-Furness area (via the Hincaster spur) to the N.E. y at Tebay. It would then be worked toward the north-east over the Stainmore line. [B. A. B

One of Tebay's Fowler 2-6-4T bankers does some light shunting between spells of duty on the bank. houses seen here were erected for L.N.W.R. employees. With the coming of the diesel, and now electr plus the closing of the Stainmore line, the *raison d'etre* of Tebay has disappeared. [B. A. B

Class 5 No. 45328, with a partly fitted freight from Carlisle to the south, passing Oxenholme No. 2 signal box, October 1956.
[B. A. Butt]

No. 46249 *City of Sheffield* and Class 5 No. 45012 at Carlisle (Citadel) in 1963. This great railway junction, at the 'scissors crossing' of four main routes, owned at one time by four separate companies, was an important division point for the L.M.S.R. and for L.M.Region, second only to Crewe. [Malcolm Dunnett]

att's little Moguls, introduced a couple of years before Nationalisation in 1948, were
gly but efficient machines, whose severely functional form tended to grow in appeal to
ost railway observers. One of their strongholds was the branch from Penrith to Keswick
nd beyond. In July 1962 No. 46433 coasts down towards the main line and Penrith with
x coaches from Keswick destined for Manchester. [Derek Cross]

close-up of No. 46203 *Princess Margaret Rose* waiting at Carlisle to take an express
to Glasgow in 1958. Behind is a 'Jubilee', No. 45698 *Achilles*, standing in the centre
d.   [Malcolm Dunnett]

A Class 5 pilots N.E. Class A2 Pacific No. 60527 *Sun Chariot* on a summer Saturday relief from Glasgow to
Leeds in 1966. On the right is another Class 5 on the goods lines. The latter are carried over the River Eden
on a new bridge erected in the Second World War at a time when the original pair of tracks seen at the
left were creating an intolerable bottleneck to the greatly increased Anglo-Scottish traffic—both freight and
passenger—in wartime.
                                                                                [Malcolm Dunnett]

Beattock bank in the summer of 1964, with a Class 5 on train 1S40, from Morecambe to Glasgow. Banking in the rear is one of the stud of 2-6-4T 'helpers' on this famous ten mile incline.
[Derek Cross]

. 43000, seen here on a freight near Kingmoor yard, north of Carlisle, after a snow fall at the end of March 6, was the first of the Class 4F moguls introduced by H. G. Ivatt in 1947. They incorporated all the latest provements in locomotive design and were later to form the basis for one of the B.R. Standard classes. e vast new marshalling yard at Kingmoor, brought into service about this time, replaced four or five mer goods yards scattered around Carlisle.
[Derek Cross]

pall of smoke from 2-6-4T No. 42195 on the last few yards to Beattock summit, before
opping away from the freight she has helped up the grade. Alone or with other banking
gines that have accumulated, she will await a path back to Beattock. The additional
st of banking operations in steam days was very considerable.   [Derek Cross]

46226
46226

No. 46226 *Duchess of Norfolk,* seen near Harthope, needs no assistance on the Beattock climb with this Crewe–Perth semi-fast in 1963. She was the last of the pre-war streamlined Stanier Pacifics to be 'defrocked' by the removal of the casing, a transformation that was carried out as and when the class went through Crewe works in the 1940's.

'Jubilee' No. 45673 *Keppel* draws away from Ayr with a Race Special returning to Glasgow whilst Class 5 No. 45022 waits in the bay with a later train for Edinburgh. The 'Jubilees' were by far the most numerous class the L.M.S.R. elected to name; having called the first one *Silver Jubilee,* they worked all round the Empire and its fringes to *Zanzibar* at No. 45638; a batch of rather assorted admirals' names was then utilised, followed by naval battles, old ex-L.N.W.R. locomotive names, warships and the like—a variety almost as entertaining as those of the 'Patriots'.

[Derek Cross]

Engaged on shunting and station pilot duties at Ayr, Ivatt Class 2 2-6-0 No. 46413 in February 1965. A sign of the times stands in the adjoining bay road—a diesel rail-bus, for which high hopes were once held for branch line rejuvenation.　　[Derek Cross]

Stanier's immortal Class 5; No. 45363 leans to the curve leading off the south end of Ribblehead viaduct in September 1963 with a fitted freight from Carlisle.   [R. H. Short]

Class 5 No. 44943 at Skipton station on 26 August 1967 with a Carlisle–Leeds parc train. Now E.E. Class 40 diesels growl over the magnificent route that is the S. & C., whe once there was the familiar beat of these 'Black Fives'.   [Derek Cros

The sturdy, fat-boilered Hughes/Fowler moguls were magnificent mixed traffic machin for their size and age. Here No. 42810 works stolidly south near Hellifield with a freight June 1957.   [R. H. Sho

In the last few years of steam, 'Jubilees' did some fine work on the Midland line from Leeds to Carlisle. No. 45646 *Napier,* seen leaving Leeds, typifies these handsome loco-motives, several of which have been preserved.   [J. R. Carter]

'Patriot' Class No. 45517 makes a good start from York with the 5.23 p.m. train to Man-chester in September 1960. One of the unnamed members of this class of 'Baby Scot' she was at this time allocated to Bank Hall shed at Liverpool.   [P. J. Lync

...ning sun illuminates ...sides of No. 45622 *...saland* as she draws ...y from Dringhouses ..., south of York, ... a fitted freight for ...shwood Heath, 24 ...gust 1963.
[P. J. Lynch]

Class 5 No. 45392 at Stockport with a mixed freight from Buxton, November 1967.
[Malcolm Dunnett]

The lines through the Peak District were Midland territory *par excellence* and the Derby-designed Class 4F 0-6-0s were commonplace both on freight and local passenger turns. Here No. 44169 *above* couples up to empty coaching stock at Buxton destined for Derby, whilst *below* No. 43967 works by with a short four-wagon freight.

[Derek Cross]

A down express hauled by Class 5 No. 45089 at Bennerley Junction, near Ilkeston, on the Trent to Chesterfield (Erewash Valley) line. It is just passing under the ex-L.N.E.R. route from Nottingham to Derby (Friargate). [P. J. Shoesmith]

Horwich mogul No. 42823 draws away from Derby with the 3.10 p.m. train to Leicester, September 1955. She was one of the class fitted with Reidinger valve gear, shedded at Burton, and is evidently suffering from a badly burned smokebox.

[P. J. Lynch]

Old but still hale and hearty, ex-Midland Class 3F 0-6-0 No. 43254 heads a Chadderdon yard–Derby (St. Mary's) freight under a signal gantry of similar vintage, June 1962.   [P. J. Lynch]

With steam shut off, Fowler 2-6-4T No. 42314 drifts beneath the imposing signal gantry at the north end of Derby with a train from Buxton, August 1962.

[P. J. Lynch]

The immortal No. 46100 *Royal Scot*, in rebuilt form, leaving Derby with a Newcastle to Bristol train, 30 March 1962. Opinions differ on whether this class was improved or not—in terms of appearance—by the rebuilding under the Stanier regime.

[P. J. Lynch]

Class 4F No. 44600, from Burton shed, was a rare visitor on the Leen Valley section of the G.N.R. when Colwick borrowed it to work the 4.30 p.m. Class H freight from Sutton-in-Ashfield to Colwick on 20 May 1957. No. 44600, seen passing Bulwell Forest, is in fact hauling two trains, the latter half of the 'consist', behind the first brakevan, being an engineer's train. [P. J. Lynch]

Steam railroading in a style seldom seen in Britain—Beyer-Garratt 2-6-6-2T No. 47982 passing Kettering with empty wagons bound for Toton yard, June 1957. The last of these 155-ton giants, built by Beyer Peacock for the L.M.S. to a design more or less based upon two Horwich moguls back to back, was withdrawn in 1958. They gave useful service for many years on coal trains between Toton and Cricklewood.   [S. Creer]

Grimy 'Jubilee' No. 45670 *Howard of Effingham* at Northampton (Castle) in Septem 1959, passing Swindon-built Class 8F No. 48427 and Ivatt 2-6-2T No. 41278.

[P. J. Shoesm

Ivatt Class 2 2-6-2T No. 41219 near Morcott, in Rutland, with a two-coach set from Stamf to Seaton.

[P. H. We

Compound 4-4-0 No. 40936 throws a pall of smoke skywards as she wrestles away from Nottingham (Midland) with a four-coach train for Sheffield. In September 1957 this was one of the last regular Compound turns in the West Midlands. [P. J. Lynch]

The ornate platform canopy at Bedford (Midland Road) throws a tracery of light and shade on to Class 3P 4-4-0 No. 40743 in a pause during carriage shunting. This was in April 1952, three months before withdrawal of this ex-Midland veteran. [P. J. Lynch]

Sunlight struggles from overhead to pierce the gloom and smoke of St. Pancras, as Compound No. 41199 starts away with the 10.50 a.m. for Bedford in April 1954—a challenge to the photographer. The immense 240ft span of the roof, covering seven platforms, made St. Pancras a major engineering wonder when it was opened in 1868. DMUs took over the Bedford service in 1960 and regular steam workings out of St. Pancras ended the following year.   [S. Creer]

A familiar backdrop of gasholder framework for a 'Jubilee' No. 45589 *Gwalior*, getting into her three-cylinder stride out of St. Pancras with an afternoon Leeds and Bradford express, May 1955.   [P. J. Lynch]

Class 4 2-6-0 No. 43031, from Derby shed, passes through Barking on an Orient Line boat train from St. Pancras to Tilbury, March 1952. The Tilbury boat trains later worked out of Fenchurch Street.   [P. J. Lynch]

M805
43031
BARKING

Class 2P 4-4-0 No. 40485 piloting 'Jubilee' No. 45620 *North Borneo* near Mill Hill with a St. Pancras–Derby express, October 1954. Derby and Crewe in harness typify the spirit of the former L.M.S.

[S. Creer]